BABIES AT THE ZOO

3

Giraffe Calves

Susan H. Gray

CHERRY LAKE PRESS

Published in the United States of America by
Cherry Lake Publishing
2395 South Huron Parkway, Suite 200, Ann Arbor, MI 48104
www.cherrylakepublishing.com

Content Advisor: Dominique A. Didier, Professor of Biology, Millersville University
Reading Advisor: Marla Conn, MS, Ed, Literacy specialist, Read-Ability, Inc.

Photo credits: ©clearviewstock/Shutterstock.com, front cover; Stacey Ann Alberts/Shutterstock.com, 1, 2; ©Jurgens Potgieter/Shutterstock.com, 4; ©Karsten Scherschanski/Shutterstock.com, 6; ©Robart Mwaiteleke/Shutterstock.com, 8; ©davegkugler/Shutterstock.com, 10; ©Michael W NZ/Shutterstock.com, 12; ©Prapaporn Somkate/Shutterstock.com, 14; ©Mikhail Semenov/Shutterstock.com, 16; ©Shiler/Shutterstock.com, 18; ©Waraphorn Aphai/Shutterstock.com, 20; Library of Congress Cataloging-in-Publication Data

Library of Congress Cataloging-in-Publication Data

Names: Gray, Susan Heinrichs, author.
Title: Giraffe calves / written by Susan H. Gray.
Description: Ann Arbor, Michigan : Cherry Lake Publishing, 2020. | Series: Babies at the zoo | Includes index. | Audience: Grades K-1.
Summary: "Read about how giraffe calves grow to be the tallest animal on land and how zookeepers take care of them. This level 3 guided reader book includes intriguing facts and adorable photos. Students will develop word recognition and reading skills while learning about how these baby animals learn and grow, what they eat, and how they socialize with each other. Book includes table of contents, glossary, index, author biographies, sidebars, and word list for home and school connection"—Provided by publisher.
Identifiers: LCCN 2019034091 (print) | LCCN 2019034092 (ebook) | ISBN 9781534158924 (hardcover) | ISBN 9781534161221 (paperback) | ISBN 9781534160071 (pdf) | ISBN 9781534162372 (ebook)
Subjects: LCSH: Giraffe—Infancy—Juvenile literature. | Zoo animals—Infancy—Juvenile literature.
Classification: LCC SF408.6.G57 G73 2020 (print) | LCC SF408.6.G57 (ebook) | DDC 599.63813/92—dc23
LC record available at https://lccn.loc.gov/2019034091
LC ebook record available at https://lccn.loc.gov/2019034092

Cherry Lake Publishing would like to acknowledge the work of the Partnership for 21st Century Learning, a Network of Battelle for Kids. Please visit http://www.battelleforkids.org/networks/p21 for more information.

Printed in the United States of America
Corporate Graphics

Table of Contents

About the Author

Susan H. Gray has a master's degree in zoology. She has written more than 150 reference books for children and especially loves writing about animals. Susan lives in Cabot, Arkansas, with her husband, Michael, and many pets.

So Tall!

What is the tallest animal on land? The giraffe! Giraffes can grow more than 18 feet (5.5 meters) tall.

Giraffes live in Africa. And some live in zoos.

Name another animal
that has spots.

A new **calf** is 6 feet (2 meters) tall. Its coat has a **pattern** of brown spots. The giraffe will keep this pattern its whole life.

Giraffes have long, skinny legs. **Newborns** try to walk on those legs. They fall down a lot at first. But they keep trying. Soon, they are running around!

Giraffes eat from trees. Adults **stretch** high up to get leaves and fruit. Babies drink milk from their mothers.

Warm Barns

At the zoo, giraffes eat hay. **Zookeepers** may also bring them **biscuits** and carrots.

Zookeepers clean the giraffe **barns**. They keep them warm in **freezing** weather. No one wants a giraffe to get sick. A sore throat would be a very big deal!

Is a 1-year-old giraffe taller than your teacher?

What a Baby!

Little giraffes begin eating leaves at about 4 months. They eat a lot. By their first birthday, they are 12 feet (3.5 meters) tall!

Giraffes are adults when they are 3 to 5 years old. Then they can have babies of their own.

Giraffe moms usually have just one baby at a time.

A baby as tall as a grown man!

Find Out More

BOOK

Dussling, Jennifer. *Giraffes.* New York, NY: Penguin Young Readers, 2016.

WEBSITE

San Diego Zoo Kids—Giraffe
https://kids.sandiegozoo.org/animals/giraffe
Learn about giraffe spot patterns, horns, and more at this site.

Glossary

barns (BARNZ) buildings that shelter giraffes and other animals
biscuits (BIS-kits) baked breads that may have other foods and healthy things mixed in
calf (KAF) the young of several large species of animals
freezing (FREEZE-ing) very cold
newborns (NOO-bornz) animals that were born recently
pattern (PAT-urn) a design or marking
stretch (STRECH) reach out
zookeepers (ZOO-kee-purz) people who take care of zoo animals

Home and School Connection

Use this list of words from the book to help your child become a better reader. Word games and writing activities can help beginning readers reinforce literacy skills.

a
about
adults
Africa
also
and
animal
another
are
around
as
at
babies
baby
barns
be
begin
big
birthday
biscuits
bring
brown
but
by
calf
can
carrots
clean
coat
deal
down
drink
eat
eating
fall
feet
first
freezing
from
fruit
get
giraffe
giraffes
grow
grown
has
have
hay
high
in
is
its
just
keep
land
leaves
legs
life
little
live
long
lot
man
may
meters
milk
moms
months
more
mothers
name
new
newborns
no
of
old
on
one
own
pattern
running
sick
skinny
so
some
soon
sore
spots
stretch
tall
taller
tallest
teacher
than
that
the
their
them
then
they
this
those
throat
time
to
trees
try
trying
up
usually
very
walk
wants
warm
weather
what
when
whole
will
would
year
years
your
zoo
zookeepers
zoos

Fast Facts

Habitat: Dry grasslands and open woodlands

Range: Africa

Average Height: Males are 19 feet (6 meters) from the ground to the top of their head. Females are 2 to 3 feet (61 to 91.5 centimeters) shorter.

Average Weight: About 2,000 pounds (907 kilograms)

Life Span: 20 to 25 years in the wild; up to 28 years in zoos

Anatomy: Giraffe horns are called ossicones. At birth, they lie flat against the head. Later, they pop up.

Behavior: Giraffes can rest and sleep standing up. In the wild, they seldom lie down.

Index